*Poems for the Young
by David McCord*

* Published in England Only

speak
up

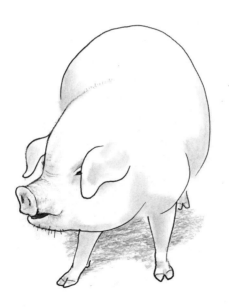

speak up

More Rhymes of the Never Was and Always Is

by David McCord

ILLUSTRATED BY MARC SIMONT

Little, Brown and Company   *Boston   Toronto*

FIRST EDITION

A number of these poems first appeared in *Cricket,
Harvard Magazine,* the *Horn Book, Yankee, Parents'
Choice* and the Boston *Globe.*
I thank the editors for permission to reprint them.

Library of Congress Cataloging in Publication Data
McCord, David Thompson Watson, 1897–
    Speak up.
    SUMMARY: Fifty poems about long words, windshield
wipers, jujubes, and other concerns of children.
    1. Children's poetry, American. [1. American
poetry] I. Simont, Marc. II. Title.
PS3525.A1655S66   811'.52   80-15260
ISBN 0-316-55517-7

BP

*Published simultaneously in Canada
by Little, Brown & Company (Canada) Limited*

PRINTED IN THE UNITED STATES OF AMERICA

To Walter D. Edmonds
in memory of
Northlands

Contents

speak
up

Look

There's something up there on the wall
That shouldn't be up there at all.

Speak Up

Lambs *bleat*
While gamboling on four springlike sprunglike feet.
Whoever thought up *bleat*?
Whoever? I repeat.

Cows *moo*?
They do for me; perhaps for you.
Look into *Webster*, though, where cows say *boo*.
Wonder what cows old Mr. Webster knew?

Horses? Resources zero. They just *neigh*.
The word is spelled that way.
Perhaps to side with *sleigh,*
Some people say.

Frogs *croak*?
I'm glad you spoke
Of that old joke:
Poetic license, which most frogs r-r-r-re*voke!*

Dogs *bark*?
Quite likely back in Noah's Ark.
How now? *Bowwow!* — especially after dark.
Leashwise they row *bowwow* in every park.

Cats howl, *meow*, spit, *purr*:
Purr when you stroke their fur.
Meow for milk — yes, sir!
Cats, of course, aren't kittens. Wish they were.

The grunts of big pigs don't have much appeal.
It's little pigs who *squeal*
And somehow make you feel
That being a pig's OK, if not ideal.

Owls *hoot?* That isn't true.
No "t." Just hoo, hoo — *hoo!*
Three, four times; maybe two.
Screech owls, though, screech at you.

Crows *caw*, they do. Their caws
Come singly, spaced. Each pause
Means something in crows' laws.
Can't tell you what, because . . .

The thrushes sing. The hermit thrush
Makes other singers sound like mush.
Clear, lonely flute — the notes don't rush.
Deep woods at dusk. You hear him? *Hush!*

But yet again:
Don't let's forget the winter wren
In Canada. So small! But when
He fills a valley, you will listen then.

Moles? Don't know what they say
In tunnels. Doesn't pay
To crawl down there by day.
It's too dark anyway.

Some far-off northern lake in June,
Night settling down to welcome the full moon.
You wait. No sound . . . no sound . . . From nowhere soon
That watery wild voice calls loon to loon.

Butterfly

Said he didn't know.
Know what?
Where he was going.
Who?
The butterfly, of course.
Butterflies don't talk. They fly.
This one talked.
You were sound asleep.
Half asleep.
Where was the butterfly?
In the field.
Where were you?
In the field.
Sound asleep?
Half asleep.
What was he doing?
Sitting against a rock.
Butterflies don't sit!
I thought you meant me.
What *was* he doing?
Standing on a weed.
Color?
Green.
I mean the butterfly.
Oh, white.

What did he look like?
A white butterfly.
Of course he looked like a white butterfly.
What do you mean?
Any spots?
Yes: orange.
Where?
On the wing tips.
Lower?
Upper.
An *Orange Tip: Anthocaris midea*.
I guess so.
I don't guess. I *know*.
OK.
So you said *what*?
"Where are you off to?"
And he said?
"Don't know. Just off."
Did you watch him?
Yes.
Where *did* he go?
To another weed.
Another?
Then another.
How did he fly?
Flapped his wings.
Who wouldn't!
I wouldn't.

OK. Flower to flower?
Weed to weed.
Kept talking?
Couldn't hear him.
Couldn't?
He mumbled.
How did he fly?
Ziggy; left-right, left-right; up, down; down, up.
Any traffic?
Grasshoppers, crickets, beetles, spiders.
I mean *flying*.
A few bugs: mosquitoes, one bumblebee, midges.
Bumblebee talked?
Bumbled something.
Just that one butterfly?
Another from the road.
What road?
Road by the field.
They met?
Zigzagged in formation.
What information?
In formation: two words.
Like two planes?
Two *slow* planes.
Naturally!
Two feet apart.
Butterflies have *six* feet.
I know. Two feet between them. Twelve if you like.

They talked?
Over the intercom.
Inaudible?
Yes.
Gee!
What?
Time for lunch.

Halloween

Samantha (call her Sam. OK?)
and her small brother Sal . . .
Why, that's a girl's name, you will say
by interrupting. Well, it may
be. I can't call him *Hal,*

for Sal he was — not Jim or Joe.
His first name puzzles me:
Salveeny — which just goes to show
that crazy parents never know
what kids will call us. He

was small and not the kind of youth
to think about his name.
Some day he'll learn how true is truth:
a baseball player G. H. Ruth
was known as Babe, whose fame

is greater than what Sal acquired
last Halloween. That's what
I started out to tell you. Tired
of interruptions, yet inspired
by spooky things, I'll not

be long. Don't go. Samantha (Sam)
and Sal her brother took
it on themselves that night to slam
no door, and answer "Here I am"
when Mother came to look

around. But they were busy all
the time with masks and sheets;
and when they stole down through the hall
they heard their mother upstairs call
"Good night!" No tricks or treats

for them! They were in bed, Mom thought.
And she? She'd gone to bed,
since Dad was out of town. She ought
of course to check on them. She'd bought
no handout stuff. Instead,

she told the children not to pay
attention to the bell.
"Just let it ring. They'll go away,
not getting anything. They'll say
some witch has cast a spell

on Halloween this year. Could be
our street is where it's cast."
That seemed to end the "Why can't *we*
go out?" Young Sal admitted *he*
was scared. But now at last

they're gone where other spooky pairs —
a few with witches' hats —
run up and down exchanging scares.
Those rascals! What a rascal wears,
all white or black as bats'

wings, doesn't matter: *who* they are
is *secret;* no one squeaks
to give himself away. A car
lights up the street; and somewhere far
and faint a dead voice speaks.

While ringing bells or running fast,
it vaguely crossed Sam's mind
though she was first, Sal (being last)
was *soundless.* Other feet rushed past —
the usual noisy kind.

Sam's had enough. Sal likewise. They
are home. Key turns the lock.
Sam creeps upstairs. Ghosts have their way
of keeping quiet. Sal can't say
"Gee whiz!" Downstairs the clock

strikes nine. Sam enters Sal's own door,
turns round. He isn't there!
She finds the switch. Heaped on the floor,
his clothes! He's sound asleep; what's more,
in bed. He didn't wear

his mask and sheet! Sam found them in
the closet with Guess what?
Mom wondered why her broom had been
upstairs! But how can Sam begin
to tell her, witch or not?

Móped

Man moped along. His Móped said:
"Put-put-put-put-put-put."
Said said reflecting in his head:
"But-but-but-but-but-but,
    Since life is measured by the wheel
    On land; in water by the keel;
    Aloft by feathers strong as steel,
Where one, if heavy, leaves a rut,
'Put-put-put-put' is nothing but
Perfection!" "In a way; not utter,"
Stuttered Móped, "stut-stut-stutter."

Roller Coaster

These roller-coaster cars, some said,
Are people sitting up in bed.
See? There they sit beyond all hope,
Positioned to roar down the slope.
So down the grade they plunge and then,
As on a wave, climb up again,
Swing sharply round some dreadful bend
Whose precipice ahead will send
Them feetfirst where you'd dare not look!
A dime or two was all it took
In *my* day for that scary run.
I don't say that it wasn't fun:
Just glad it's over with and done.

Well, roller-coaster days are gone
Most places. If you've not been on
One, nothing much that I can say
Will help you understand the way
It's not exactly you who take
The ride on wheels which have no brake:
Your stomach does the traveling,
The rest of you unraveling
Behind it, like a ball of twine
(While spider-legs run up your spine)
That's rolling off a roof with no
One there to catch it down below.

But worst, of course, is each slow climb
To heights you couldn't call sublime,
Where suddenly you round that curve
Precisely as you lose your nerve.

In Portland, Oregon, a park
Stood close to us, and after dark
In summer I could hear the screams
From roller coasting, see the gleams
Of lights cut off by cars that swung
Across them. That's when stomachs hung
In space apart from bodies shot
Straight down the rails. If I had got
To sleep, sometimes I dreamt *my* bed
Was on that roller coaster, led
By other beds ahead, and mine
Unrolling like that ball of twine
Up on the roof, as in my sleep
I gathered speed to make the leap,
And some hot night was broken by
A single yell . . . and I . . . and I . . .

Now if you like this sort of thing,
And come back safe, give me a ring.
But if you *don't* come back, don't bother;
Not to hear at all, I'd rather.

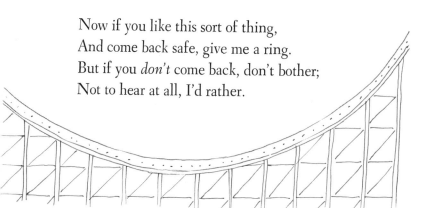

Limericks

There's an ant on the front windowsill.
He is searching for something. He's still
    Going up, down, left, right.
    Who could look on his plight
And not open the sash, as I will?

There was life in the dead tree that fell
In the night in the storm. Need I tell
    You I found it all runny
    With bees? Saved the honey.
The bees? In a hive, doing well.

Think of darkness. Then think of the mole
In his tunnel: black, black as black coal.
    But the traffic is light,
    And the weather's all right,
And the tunnel is free — there's no toll.

There's a lift up aloft for the wing
Of some glider that's likely to bring
    It in range of my kite.
    Cut the string? Well, I might;
But I'd rather hear something go *ping!*

Just a mouse in the wainscot, they say.
Not a *waistcoat*, a *wainscot*. OK?
    Are there more in the house?
    Does each one have a mouse?
What's he do there? Just eat? Sleep? Or play?

Take the dolphin: as smooth and as slick
And as smart as the dickens. No trick
    He can't do. Leap and dive?
    He's a rainbow alive:
Spick-and-span, spick-and-span, span-and-spick.

Though the termite be sharp as they come,
He is highly unwelcome to some.
    Is your house made of wood?
    That's his picnic: a good
Old removable feast, crumb by crumb.

Ask a squirrel, when he's cracking a nut,
"Is it good?" "It is anything but,"
    He replies between teeth,
    As they shatter the sheath:
Open shut, open shut, open shut.

The turtle, of course, has a shell.
Yet so very few people can tell
    Me those plates in three rows
    On his back, like your toes
Have a number. Thirteen? You do well.

Let me weigh what to say of the bat;
You can't hold him and give him a pat;
    Still, there's no other thing
    With a leatherlike wing
In the world. There! At least I've said *that!*

So you found some fresh tracks in the snow?
And what made them? You say you don't know?
    Were they two pairs of skis?
    Rabbits down on their knees?
Or a skunk with a splint on his toe?

There's a bittern that booms in a bog
Where he's standing in front of a log.
    But the log doesn't mind:
    Says he's *always* behind.
"Hear that horn?" "Yes." "I don't see no fog."

An artist who set up his easel
Attracted a skunk and a weasel,
    One badger, two deer,
    Which to him wasn't queer.
What'll do for his subject? Why, these'll.

"One egg in the nest of that crow
Wasn't laid by the owner." "How so?"
    "Why, a low-flying duck
    Dropped it in there for luck."
"Will the duckling be happy?" "Don't know."

So your phone discontinues to buzz?
Tomorrow they'll see that it does.
     And if this isn't clear —
     As it isn't, I fear —
Who will know what it is that it was?

Have you ever reflected on green
As the dominant color between
     Earth and sky? How the leaf
     Holds your eyes like a thief?
In the country, what else have you seen?

On the Slope

Pulled something,
He said.
(He was pulling a sled
Up the big hill ahead.)
Pulled a muscle, I guess.
Yes, a muscle,
And Gus'll
Be limping.

The kid
On the sled
Said he *did*
Limp. So this'll
Be it. Likely Gus'll
Go home.
Got to hustle
Myself! Cold as Nome
Where kids whistle
Downhill
For the thrill;
But it's tough
Climbing back
Up the track —
Huff and puff.
Going strong?
Had enough?
Well, so long.

Groundhog

A woodchuck is a groundhog.
You can say
A groundhog is a woodchuck —
Either way.

He makes his burrow cozy
Underground.
Two doors it has. He knows he
Won't be found.

He eats what's in your garden —
Steals, that is.
He never begs your pardon.
What's not his

Is tastier and fresher
Than sweet hay.
He has no scythe or thresher;
But you'd say

He leaves a little plot of
Land as bare
As harvesters — men not of
Him aware

While they are in the corn or
Milking cows.
He doesn't even warn or
Ask them, "How's

It going?" while they're busy
With their chores.
But is *he* busy! *Is* he!
His two doors

Are always open night or
Day. He's gone
Before they catch the blighter,
Or catch on

To what he's up to, eating
Secretly.
His whistle is no greeting:
It means *Flee!*

Still, groundhog's at our service
Once a year.
Not sleepy, no, nor nervous,
He'll appear

On February second
On the dot.
As if someone had beckoned,
Out he'll trot

To see if he can see his
Shadow cast.
If he *can* see it, he is
Gone; and fast

Asleep before we come to
Realize
Spring's six weeks off! It's dumb to
Think he lies.

Farther and Further

Farther is distance and *further* is time.
I ask, does your nickel resemble my dime?
No, it doesn't. And "a" doesn't look like a "u";
But in *farther* or *further?* Well, either will do,
People say. *They are wrong!* Look at *farther,* where *far*
Ought to tell you at once that the moon or the star
Is *farther* away than that bird overhead.
Furthermore, *further* thought to what I have just said
Means you'll take a few minutes of time — two or three.
Would you give *farther* thought to it? No? You agree?
Farther thought sounds plain silly. You wouldn't be caught
Saying *that,* or you're *farther* from me than *I* thought.

Traffic Lights

Green is instant;
So is red.
One says, *Go it!*
One, *Stop dead!*
But red and yellow
Mix their talk
Of automation.
They say, WALK!

The Octopus

The octopus, if he could speak,
would say his name is from the Greek,
spelled *oktopous,* eight-footed one:
Eight feet to move with, not to run,
yet mighty useful to explore
and find what he is looking for
down in the dark — not *really* look
so much as *feel* for. In my book
no other living thing can eat
the way he does with all eight feet —
not eight at once of course: the one
that grabbed his victim on the run
across the ocean floor or took
one swimming just the way you crook
your finger round a pencil or
the brass knob on your own front door.

The elephant, if he were sunk
beneath the sea, would have his trunk —
one tentacle, let's say. Well, eight
times *that's* an octopus. Those great
long trunks or feelers, down their length
have rows of suction cups, the strength
of wrestlers writhing on the mat.
Would eight half nelsons lay you flat?

You bet they would!
                     I'll tell you why
they say the octopus is shy:
sun dancing on the surface wave
can't reach him deep down in his cave.
He's shy the way a spider is:
the web is hers, the cave is his;
and each does better out of sight
of fly or fish, to catch them. Right?
You feel you'd like to feel the feel
of one? Pick up a snake or eel:
one creepy and one slippery, so
just try them barefoot with your toe.
Don't try an octopus! The Greek
word doesn't warn you of his beak.

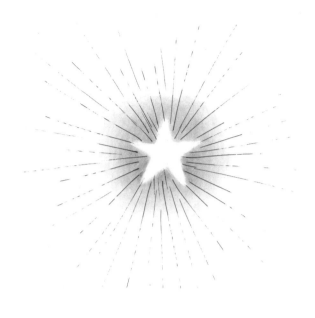

Who Can Say?

A dump truck full of jelly beans?
You wonder where it dumps 'em?
A dump truck full of tangerines?
You wonder where it plumps 'em?
We hear of curious things like this —
Big chances much too good to miss.
Such things are *always* out of reach,
Like one last apple or one peach
Quite visible up high, too far.
We think that way about a star.

Worm

That lonely worm upon the lawn!
He squirms. Must wonder what goes on
Down in his tunnel flooded out
By rain the clouds poured from a spout.
It won't be long before he *could*
Go back; but he's up here for good —
Or bad, if robin sees him there.
He's lost, and doesn't know just where
He surfaced. Soon the sun will dry
Him dead. But no; he's caught the eye
Of Hilda, soaked, and running by.

Well, Hilda, spotting him, did not
Quite see the croquet wicket, got
Her foot in it, fell flat, and tore
The wicket out, which left a door
Wide open on a hole close to
Big squirmy worm. What would he do?
Do? Guess! He went right down it fast.
The cold, wet robin, hopping past
Had caught a glimpse of juicy him;
Stopped, thrust his bill down. But the rim
Held firm enough. The worm in his
Own element! Fat, thin, he is
There, inching home through soggy sod,
Safe as a pea inside its pod.

The Windshield Wipers' Song

Late pretty late
Late pretty late
What held you up?
What held you up?
Rained cats and dogs
Rained cats and dogs
Car got a wash
Car got a wash

Weather says sleet
Weather says sleet
Low on the gas?
Low on the gas?
Look at the gauge
Look at the gauge
Yes you forgot
Yes you forgot

Get me new blades
Get me new blades
How's it inside?
How's it inside?
Can't make you out
Can't make you out
Turn me on fast
Turn me on fast

That's better faster
That's better faster
Car's on your tailgate
Car's on your tailgate
Try the brakes easy
Try the brakes easy
Guy must be crazy
Guy must be crazy
Guy must . . .

From the Persian

You know *no* Persian words?
Oh, yes, you do:
Caravan and *paradise*, for two.
Did Poe know Persian words?
Of course he did!
He kept some in a box. Lift up the lid,
Try *tulip, julep, jujube,* and *bazaar;*
Diván, verandah, jasmine, kiosk, scimitar;
Sugar, turban, taffeta, pistachio,
And *tamarind.* How many *don't* you know?
Roc, parasang, or *Mazda?* You know *roc:*
Enormous flightless bird — not out of stock;
Just never (you may look him up) existed!
Can you add another word to those I've listed?
I doubt it.
How about it?

Word Music

"Silly Sylvia's in the salvia."
Flo's for that. But Joe
Proposes "Rose is where her nose is."
Which is better? Flo's is? Joe's is?
"Mebbie . . ." Debby eyes her wiser
Sister who tried *"I'd*
Say, 'Andy's candy made Jill ill.' "
"Vote *for* it, Flo?" "No?" "Phil?"

                                     Yes, Phil
And Phil's affiliate, Will, will.

Mystery

"I have to go now." Letter isn't signed,
And somehow, rather, I begin to wonder.
The writer *did* say, "You are very kind."
But "have to go now": *That* sticks in the mind!

Who had to go? And *where?* Up north? Down under?
"I have to go now." Letter isn't signed.
Who had to go so quickly, leave behind
An unsigned letter? Not a *fatal* blunder:

The writer *did* say, "You are very kind."
Perhaps I *had* been, though I'll never find
The reason. After lightning comes no thunder.
"I have to go now." Letter isn't signed.

And no address: just silence underlined.
The postmark was all blurred: it looked like "Munder."
The writer did say, "You are very kind."
So there's my treasure — not a pirate's plunder;

Nothing to prove my world is torn asunder.
"I have to go now." Letter isn't signed.
The writer *did* say, "You are very kind."

Jujubes

Drupaceous fruit,
Rhamnaceous tree:
Produce them jujubes
Just for me!
Projuice 'em juicy as can be.

Skyviews

1. The Sun
Unbuttoned button
in the sky's blue shirt,
with not one hole to hold it.

2. The Moon
Thin slice of melon,
half an orange,
big round fresh Brie cheese
on a lakeside summer night.

Midsummer

The river's high, the clouds are low;
Some swallows fly, and in a row
Six ducks swim, cycling from the shore.
Is that enough? I can't say more.

But yes, I can: I failed to note
One oarless and abandoned boat
Chained to a tree just halfway up
The bank, rust-water in a cup

Back toward the stern near five dead worms
In bilge. Long since they lost their squirms.
An old fishhook with broken gut
Hangs stuck beneath a thwart, one cut

Of short silk line attached to it.
Some water striders flit, skit-skit,
Below the gunnels where a newt —
A yellow one — floats past the root

Of time's dead tree. The striders' feet
In saucers skip their always neat
Geometry of lines and angles.
Now a small green inchworm dangles

From a thread I cannot see.
Well, that's the picture — all for free.

Those Double Z's

Razzle
dazzle
nuzzle
drizzle
guzzle
sizzle
sozzle
frizzle
muzzle
nozzle
puzzle

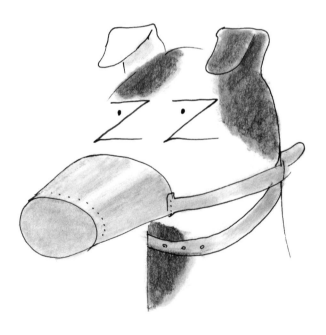

Rathers

What bothers me are rathers such as these:
"I'd rather not" amounts to a disease.
"I'd rather this than that" — This pie? That cheese?

"It's rather cold," they say. Of course! You'll freeze!
"I rather think you will" suggests he sees
Straight through you: that you *won't;* no pretty please.

"I'd rather not discuss it" puts the squeeze
On someone acting like a dog with fleas.
The English *"Rather!"* means the man agrees.

"I'd like it rather better with two *t*'s"
Sounds too polite, too anxious to appease.
"Seems rather funny . . ." *What?* Forgot his skis? . . .

You haven't heard? . . . No honey? All those bees? . . .
How queer! These "rather funny's" grow on trees.
We shoot the language while we shoot the breeze.

"Seems rather funny . . ." Tweezers just won't tweeze?
"Seems rather funny . . ." *Uno:* He's . . . or She's . . .

Witch's Broom

Witch enters tool and potting shed,
Looks at her broom and shakes her head,
Slips down to the hardware store instead
Of flying. "Want a broom," she said.

"A broom? You'd like perhaps a small
Fat model, since you're not too tall?
We've others. Let me show them all.
For some, of course, there's not much call.

"This broom is special: curb and bridle.
Hangs by the reins, you see, when idle.
Not a broom to prance and sidle —
Not at all. You'll find the ride'll

"Be quite smooth and safe. You'll purr
Along." Man looks quite sharp at her.
"You ride sidesaddle? You prefer
A whip or crop? Perhaps a spur?"

"I use a spell. The spell I cast
On any broom's enough to last
The night. I don't ride far or fast
Like famous witches of the past."

"I see. But if you need to zoom,
We have a new gas-model broom
I'll show you in the other room:
Quite silent, like a flying tomb.

"It corners well; and anyhow
It runs on bottled stardust. Cow
Jumped over Moon: but you'll allow
That's myth, not competition now."

"No, thanks! A plain broom does for me.
My cat is used to that, for she
Just hops on when I crook my knee.
She navigates, for cats can see

"Much better than a witch at night.
You'll let me make a practice flight?
You know I have to hold on tight."
"A bridle, though, may help." "It might."

The broom is bought. The witch pays cash.
The old broom goes out with the trash;
But from the town dump (which is rash)
Takes off. Who knows where it will crash?

Ladybug

We say *ladybug;*
The English don't.
They say *ladybird;*
But I just won't.
    I'm sure they know a bug is *not*
    A bird in any sense.
    Why, lots and lots of bugs have got
    Their wings at no expense;
    But they are bugs, though, just the same —
    The ladybug no less.
    And anyhow, I like the name
    And anyhow, I guess
    Of ladybird some haven't heard.
    But now they have, I hope the word
    Will make each one confess:
We say *ladybug;*
The English don't.
They say *ladybird;*
But I just won't.

Rain

What a day! Does it *rain!* Is it rainy!
Trust Laney and Janey: both out.
Take the lawn: full of pools where it puddled,
Befuddled fat worms squirm about.
A ditch freshly dug overflowing,
Now showing such maculate mud:
Aren't Janey and Laney smack in it
The minute they see it in flood?
No socks and no shoes make it easy
In squeezy black ooze to have fun.
Down the ditch they plunge sopping, no stopping,
With whopping freefalls while they run.
Have you ever been wet in a better
Or wetter way? Out with a splash,
To the pond and the springboard — you guessed it:
They test it, dive off in a flash,
Swimming clean as a whistle — why whistles,
Like thistles, are clean, I don't know;
Scramble out with warm rain on their faces.
No traces of mud, home they go.
"It's raining," say people, complaining,
Regaining their seats by the screen.
Did they never know rain can be heaven
At seven? at eight? at thirteen?

Gold

Most backyard leaves grown old,
I count three turned to gold.
The oak went brown, the sumach red;
The beech in bronze will hang its head.
No change in them foretold
Just what this maple still unshed
Could not — would not — withhold:
Sun's thimbleful of gold returning
Gold so you can see it burning.

Cricket

When a cricket chirps fast, it is hot.
When he chirps rather slowly, it's not.
    Does he chirp the advance
    Of a cloudburst? No chance!
Take your pick: fast or slow's all he's got.

If at math you don't rate as a whiz,
Want to know what the temperature is?
    Count his chirps, one by one;
    Thirteen seconds — you're done.
Then add forty. Your answer is his.

Spittlebug

The spittlebug?
A *little* bug.
When he's a nymph, he spits
A ball of foam and makes his home
Inside it. See it? It's
on stems of plants, on grasses.
There is nothing to make passes
At it: not a bird, I guess,
Would care to stick his bill in goo —
I wouldn't now, I think, would you? —
To search through such a mess.

Riddle-Me Rhyme

Riddle-me, Riddle-me, Ree,
An owl is in that tree.
Riddle-me, Riddle-me, Ro,
He's there and he won't go.
Riddle-me, Riddle-me, Ree,
"I'm staying here," says he.
Riddle-me, Riddle-me, Ro,
"Caw-caw," caws the crow.
Riddle-me, Riddle-me, Ree,
An owl by day can't see.
Riddle-me, Riddle-me, Ro,
But he can hear the crow.
Riddle-me, Riddle-me, Ree,
Not *one* crow: now but three.
Riddle-me, Riddle-me, Ro,
Now five or six or so.
Riddle-me, Riddle-me, Ree,
Nine, ten crows round that tree.
Riddle-me, Riddle-me, Ro,
Now forty. He won't go.
Riddle-me, Riddle-me, Ree,
How deafening crows can be!
Riddle-me, Riddle-me, Ro,
The owl's still saying "No!"

Riddle-me, Riddle-me, Ree,
Did something leave the tree?
Riddle-me, Riddle-me, Ro,
You'll have to ask a crow.
Riddle-me, Riddle-me, Ree,
The crows are following he. . . .
Riddle-me, Riddle-me, Ro,
Are following *him*.

I know.

Joggers

To see his jogs
You'd think he runs
On clockwork cogs.
His two small sons
Need three to equal
His long stride;
And then the sequel
Three.
      Beside
Them pants a spaniel,
Far too fat.
His name is Daniel.
Good name, *that!*
One Daniel in
The Lions' Den
Had luck to win,
Got out, and *then*
He jogged or ran
Back home. You, Pup,
Now, while you can,
Should give it up.

How to Learn to Say
a Long, Hard Word

1.

I tried to say it; *how* I tried!
I did it. Now I'll be your guide.
mucopolysaccharide:
Easy as on ice to slide —
mew-
ko-
polly-
Sacka-
ride.
It's *not* a word you'll use or need to know;
but *all* long words break down this way, and so:

2.

Another word, but less, far less, sensational:
sixteen letters. Try it: *multiplicational.*
Very easy. *Look for rhymes.*
Say it over several times.
A station *wagon* rhymes with *dragon.*
So does *station* rhyme with *cation.*
Not sensational, as I said;
just break it up the way it's read.
OK, now?
Here is how —

multi-
plick-
A-
shun-
al.

> You won't need this; but I'm about
> to show you three long words with clout.

3.

First, here's a word that you *can* use:
a word in which you'll take some pride.
It's not a *tough* word to refuse,
like *mucopolysaccharide,*
for *discombobulate,* as you may know,
means simply to upset you, *really* throw
you out of gear, or off the trolley. Stated
plainly, *discombobulated*
is what *you are at times!* A fine old word
in mockery of Latin — not absurd.
Two syllables, not looked at one by one,
suggest a *disco — not the way it's done.*
It's

dis-
comm-
Bob-
you-
late.

I hope you see
it's *Bob* who gets the accent. You agree?

4.

This word of the past, and far from dead:
sockdolager is easily said.
Use as you wish:
"What a *whopping* big fish,"
he says of your prize?
Well, to give it real size,
so it bugs out his eyes,
say,

> sock-
> *Dollage-*
> err.

> > *That* will surprise!

5.

Limicoline, an adjective, describes
some shore birds, like sandpipers — little tribes
that trot along the curvy line of foam
when tides are running out or coming home.
They skip, you know, like tiny clockwork toys
whose legs crisscross, crisscross, but make no noise.
Limicoline means "living in the mud,"
not in the *earth* like turnip, beet, or spud:
lim-
Mick-
a-
line.

> There's something fresh and clean
> about the *sound* of it. See what I mean?

6.

Persnickety: a fussy word, means just
exactly that: and if you ever fussed
to make exact and perfect as could be
what you were working at, then you are he
or she who loves perfection. You are blessed
beyond all praise, for you will never rest
with doing anything you undertake
to do unless you do it well. You'll make
your mark in life, and be unsatisfied
with sloppiness in those who take no pride
in doing *anything* the way it should
be done. *Persnickety* means you are good
at absolutely everything you do.
Be glad if what I say of you is true.
Purr-
Snick-
a-
tee.

> If someone calls you that,
> it means you'll hit what you are aiming at.

7.

Lollapalooza,
to roll on the tongue,
is another jim gem
of a word for them
who go wild, let's say,
on a fast double play;
spot a hornets' nest hung
from the branch of a tree;
see a mile run won
in three fifty-three;
take a picnic, even —
it just might be —
when the day and the sky
and the pie and the cake
and the swim in the lake
(with nobody sick)
were all (hope to die)
what no money can buy!
You can say it was *jake,*
you can say it was *slick,*
or *fantastic,* or choose a
big *lollapalooza!*
Lolla-
pal-
Ooze-
a.

    That's what it meant
to you: *lollapalooza* — best day ever spent!

Earwig

The earwig? He's a slender small black bug
Who has a pair of pincers for a tail.
You will not find him underneath the rug
Or in a shell abandoned by a snail.

You will not find him in a person's ear —
No use to ask someone if you may look!
It's in the garden where earwigs appear,
And not between the pages of a book.

He wasn't born to keep house in a wig;
Nor should you worry when you brush your hair.
Myself, I find him clinging to a twig
Or on a leaf; not any other where.

He gets his name from having once been thought
To try to reach man's head in through his ear —
Though doing so, he never once was caught.
The Anglo-Saxon language, which sounds queer,

Has given us his *wig*: about the same
As *wicga*, meaning *insect*. You can guess
To this and that some other silly name
Has stuck. It has! It has indeed. Yes, yes.

To Walk in Warm Rain

To walk in warm rain
    And get wetter and wetter!
To do it again —
To walk in warm rain
    Till you drip like a drain.
To walk in warm rain
    And get wetter and wetter.

Legs

When I asked the class, "How many legs
on a housefly?" someone once said,
"Whose house?" So the laughter led
to laughter and "That doesn't matter."
One girl did come up then with "Two"
(the number of yolks in two eggs)
as if she could hear the clatter
of heels on the kitchen table.
Hands always go up for "Four." So many
have actually seen a cow, horse, dog,
or cat; and so aren't able
to see horse, cow, cat, dog, or any
fly with more. Four legs *look* stable.
But one or two shout "Six" — a view
quite bold. I hold with six as true;
glad just in knowing (perhaps) who really *knew*.

"How many legs has a spider?" The class
will respond like a shot: "A spider? *Eight!*"
which is right, of course. There's not
(as with the housefly question, alas)
the least — not any — hesitation:
no look to see if I disagree. And why?

Why, because there is something about a spider
that scares us: a queer up-spine sensation
we have of fear at sight of the hourglass spot
on the common (too common) "black widow." We know
the furry legs of the black tarantula; know
the trapdoor part of those myriad lovely webs
on the grass after rain — webs radar-scanned
by their owners — who wove them — as planned.
We all have watched while enveloping spiders took
in the fly in their claws — it seems always these are "she's";
and the crooked-crawl horrible laddery-look
of eight legs as they clamber down
the ladder. The adder and rattlesnake have no
legs; but the spider has eight. If then her mate
is not right there beside her, and cannot divide her
attention: good reason. It's him she ate.

Awake

Who is first up?

I am, said Snail.
Dawn's not so pale
As my sticky trail.

I am, said Bird.
It was me you heard
When no one had stirred.

I am, said Fox.
I need no clocks.
I sleep in my socks.

I am. A Raccoon
Would just as soon
Get up with the moon.

I am, said Crow,
Cawing as I go.
Where? How do *I* know?

I am, said Rooster.
Dawn's old top booster,
I be. Least I useter.

I am, said Worm.
I emerge. I squirm,
So the Robins affirm.

I am, said Trout.
If you have any doubt,
Ask a fly that's out.

I am, said Cow.
Had my breakfast. How
Is *your* cud right now?

I am, said Hare,
In your garden where
There is lettuce to spare.

I am, said Bat;
But I'll bet my hat
None notices that.

Well, I'm *not,* said Mole.
I'm down in my hole
Where it's black as coal.

In the End

So when the bugs take over,
Shall we charge it off to chance
That the universal victor will
Be armies of the ants?

I'd much prefer the ladybugs,
The lightning bugs, the crickets,
Who spend their droll, delightful lives
In hayfields and in thickets.

I wouldn't mind the bees: the bears
And I are hipped on honey.
I'd hate to think of spider,
Wasp, or mantis in the money;

Or beetles, earwigs, aphids, lice;
Ticks, flies; or gnats and fleas;
Or worms and slugs and other bugs.
Mosquitoes? No thanks, please!

Not katydids, grasshoppers, locusts,
Shrill cicadas — *No!*
Most bugs that fiddle, jump, or run.
Cockroaches? Out they go!

Still, dragonflies have color: they'd
Go easy on the eyes;
Except, you must remember, man
Is dead, and his demise

Means who would see or care? There will
Be no one to lament
His passing. Like the dinosaur, he
Came and saw and went.

But ants, ahead of all of us,
Long since were underground.
The termites, cretomasters, leaf
Ants, fire ants, all abound

The round earth over. Old as
Amber, fossil ants preserve
The likeness of that tireless race
To tell us they deserve

The heritage which, I predict,
They jolly well may get.
Of that, though, we'll not know; and so,
Not knowing, can't regret.

Perhaps

Perhaps I didn't,
Perhaps I did;
Perhaps I just forgot
The lid.